THE
SIX-CORNERED
SNOWFLAKE

ALSO BY JOHN FREDERICK NIMS

P O E T R Y

Five Young American Poets: Third Series (with others) (1944)

The Iron Pastoral (1947)

A Fountain in Kentucky (1950)

Knowledge of the Evening (1960)

Of Flesh and Bone (1967)

The Kiss: A Jambalaya (1982)

Selected Poems (1982)

Zany in Denim (1990)

T R A N S L A T I O N

Euripides' Andromache (in *Complete Greek Tragedies*) (1959)

The Poems of St. John of the Cross (1959; rev., 1969; third ed., 1979)

Sappho to Valéry: Poems in Translation (1971; rev., 1980; enlarged, 1990)

P R O S E

Western Wind: An Introduction to Poetry (1974; rev., 1983)

A Local Habitation: Essays on Poetry (1985)

E D I T I O N S

The Poem Itself (with others) (1960)

Ovid's *Metamorphoses: The Arthur Golding Translation* (1965)

James Shirley's *Love's Cruelty* (1980)

The Harper Anthology of Poetry (1981)

John Frederick Nims

THE
SIX-CORNERED
SNOWFLAKE
and Other
Poems

A NEW DIRECTIONS BOOK

PS
3527
.I863
55
1990

Copyright © 1983, 1984, 1985, 1986, 1987, 1988, 1989, 1990 by John Frederick Nims

ACKNOWLEDGMENTS

Grateful acknowledgment is made to the following books and magazines in which some of the poems here were first published: *The American Scholar, The Atlantic, The Bennington Review, The Bread Loaf Anthology of Contemporary American Poetry, The Georgia Review, Grand Street, The Kentucky Poetry Review, The New Criterion, New Directions in Prose & Poetry 52, Poetry, The Sewanee Review, The Southern California Anthology, The Yale Review.*

Sincere thanks are due also to the John Simon Guggenheim Foundation for the Fellowship during which several of the poems in this volume were written.

Manufactured in the United States of America
New Directions Books are printed on acid-free paper.
First published clothbound and as New Directions Paperbook 700 in 1990
Published simultaneously in Canada by Penguin Books Canada Limited

Library of Congress Cataloging-in-Publication Data

Nims, John Frederick, 1913–
    The six-cornered snowflake and other poems / John Frederick Nims.
        p.   cm.—(New Directions paperbook; 700)
    ISBN 0–8112–1143–6 (alk. paper). —ISBN 0–8112–1144–4 (pbk.:
alk. paper)
      I. Title.
PS3527.I863S5   1990   90–33222
811'.54—dc20   CIP

New Directions Books are published for James Laughlin
by New Directions Publishing Corporation,
80 Eighth Avenue, New York 10011

Contents

THE SIX-CORNERED SNOWFLAKE   1

GRAVITY   13

KEEPING CHANGE   15

THE SHAPE OF LEAVES   18

TRICK OR TREAT   19

FROM THE RAPIDO: LA SPEZIA–GENOVA   20

IN VENICE, THE LIGHT AIRS   21

WATER MUSIC   22

DROPPING THE NAMES   26

THE WINE OF ASTONISHMENT   28

CLOSED FOR RESTORATION   34

HOSPITAL BREAKFAST: WITH GRACE AFTER   35

ELEGY   37

MÉLISANDE AT THE KALEIDOSCOPE   39

POETRY WORKSHOP (FIRST SEMESTER)   40

THE CLOSING TOMB   42

PALINODE   43

DANTE: AL POCO GIORNO . . .   45

NIAGARA   47

Notes   50

Afterword: Some Notes on Form and Formalism   53

. . . εἰς τὸν ποιητὴν οὐρανοῦ καὶ γῆς . . .

THE SIX-CORNERED SNOWFLAKE

Strena, seu De Nive Sexangula . . .

*

The

snows

curleycue

in slow pendulous

* pavane, half lured to heaven yet, until *

they too concede to earth, drift and accrue

on rugged roofs like plowlands pitched

at odds, akimbo, a mottled-lavender

jumble of old-gold corrugated tile

lofting its crown of thorny towers

over a Prague still Gothic (1610),

Prague not yet voluted with baroque,

aspiring still: see many-steepled Týn!

church-spire on spire like missiles packed

* all zeroed in on heaven. Zigzag streets *

crevassing seesaw

gables all

round

Týn

*

```
                    *
                  Now
                 zoom
              in on "the
           incomparable man"
 *    (said Einstein) Kepler, hazy eyes ablink,    *
      steel mind dividing all heaven like a pie,
      whanging the startled orbits till they
      rang! Now, this December noon, he's
      trudging in snow to see the emperor
      out thru the escutcheoned tower's
      stone  calendar  of  warrior-saints,
      helms, haloes diamonded with snow,
      then  on  to  the  half-mile  windiness of
      bridge hurdling the winter river in sixteen
 *    soaring stone leaps, to couch beneath the    *
              castled heights of
                 Hradčany
                  in the
                  sky
                    *
```

```
                          *
                        The
                       steep
                     question-
                mark crook of road
     *    tires him; halfway he'll lounge a while,    *
         look back on the quirky panoramic roofs of
         a two-part city the great river splits:
            yonder's the Old Town, Staré Město;
            here Malá Strana strays: ma la la la
            K. croons it, the musical Czech name,
            eye straying to snow on his coat—
            while Emperor Rudolf, head in clouds,
          frets in his fabulous attic of retorts,
         zodiacs spyglass crucible rubies clocks
     *   Brueghels Dürer—Arcimboldo: royal phiz    *
                   abloom in bulbous
                      fruit thru
                        goblin
                         art
                          *
```

                            *
                           But
                          today
                       the Royal
                  Astronomer's late,
   *   hunched there, his mind aswirl with more   *
      than whimwhams of an emperor—all bemused
        by signatures of something from above:
          the dædal snowflake crystaling in six.
            Old thunders roll: "Hast entered
            into the treasures of the snow?"
            Not yet; but mind is given to know;
            the great world to be known. Why six?
          Perhaps no reason but exuberant joy?
        Pattern's a pleasure; often nature plays
   *   not for rude truth but loveliness of line: *
                  item: this Gothic
                      mandala's
                       set of
                        six

                            *

                               *
                              Out
                             of the
                           blue, his
                        thoughts like snow
*   flocking in flurries: the black savagery   *
       of upper air blanched to this flossiness?
       Is snow among the amenities of nature,
       falling in figures? With Euripides, he
       remembers how Polyxena at the tomb,
       snowy throat bared, chin tilted for
       the sword that trembled more than
       she, was "careful to fall decently,"
       still minding her skirt now hieroglyphed
       with blood. He dreams: over roofs of Prague
*   a pale girl floating amid geometries . . .   *
                        Fantastical—he's
                          our myriad-
                            minded
                             man

                               *

*

Not

above

a juggler's

way with words, as:

* in swank of scholastic Latin *nix* is *snow;* *

but, in his burlier German, *nichts* is *nothing.*

Ergo: this snow, like all the world, is

only a pale chemise on nothingness.

You doubt? He'll quote you Persius:

"O curas hominum, O quantum est in

rebus inane." Hollow hopes of men!

One solace though: "A living death

is life without philosophy." Or life

without its drollery: he'll wink at snow's

* raunchy role in folklore. "A snowflake *

got me with child,"

naughtier

ladies

say

*

*

One
grouch,
cornuted
so, totes the tad
* south to dispose of, miming in mock woe,   *
"Your snowflake baby melted in the sun."
Feet shuffle in the decencies of nature.
Meanwhile K. rakes among six-angled
sorts for a clue. In pomegranate?
honeycomb? Prime diamonds mined in
wash of gravel favor octahedrons,
compacted to six peaks—to six, eureka!
Here's earth and sky attuned, a same
sign from each, extruded from blue flues of
* long extinct volcanos; from blue choirs   *
of heaven, the two
choraling
raptly
six

*

　　　　　　　*
　　　　　　All
　　　　　primal
　　　　　forms are
　　　　hieroglyph: *forma*
*　　means *soul* for the philosophers, as for　*
　　John Dee, sometime astronomer in Prague,
　　who saw once in this mirror of a world
　　God as "the *Form* of forms." So Kepler
　　dreams. To find why forms from *Form*
　　scintillate, hover, hold in harmony
　　the universe—his passion's there,
　　his "only delight." Blear of eye, he
　　unriddled optics, made heaven an aviary
　　of singing planets, bizarre cage in cage,
*　coped with his Starry Messenger, Galileo,　*
　　　　but never rightly
　　　　　solved the
　　　　　why of
　　　　　six

　　　　　　*

*

Nor
solved
the riddle
of himself, a soul
* "like sweet bells jangled": his mother a *
mumbling witch, father a traipsing bravo;
wife in the dumps, babes wailing; great
Tycho dabbing his patchy nose of gold;
feast or famine from the emperor;
a body of scabs and rashes—boils
raw in the saddle, so must trudge
afoot after surly printers set to sue;
then arson, looting, thirty years of war;
his grave obliterated—*this* man attuned
* the universe itself in *Harmonice Mundi*? *
made of his quaint
delusions
music
too

*

*

We

dream

in neurons.

Form lost in forms,

* a blizzard of data blinds our monitors. *

Today, more knowing, we know less. But know

less more minutely. A schoolboy could

dazzle poor Kepler with his chemistry,

chat of molecular bonds, how H:Ö:H

freezes to crystal, the six struts

magnetized by six hydrogen nuclei

(so goes a modern Magnificat to snow)

its six electrical terminals alluring

a bevy of sprightly molecules from out of

* weather's nudge and buffeting, the tips *

culling identical

windfalls

of fey

air

*

```
                        *
                       Six:
                      every
                     petal in
                  symmetry. And yet
    *    no flake like any other, each enjoying    *
         a different taste of heaven's variation:
         warm, windy, wet, by millimeters, mingle,
           freezing molecules till they encode
            the millisecond's dharma. Dare we
            say, so with us? One muffled moon,
            candlelit hands, a half-caught sob,
           icon, child's sled, or horseshoe nail
         can reassign the history of our days.
         "From what Paradisal imagineless metal too
    *    costly for cost" are snowflakes wrought?    *
               one poet lyricked,
                   not quite
                    in K.'s
                     way
                        *
```

*

He's

had no

truck with

such "imagineless"

* commodities; he loves hang, heft, and edge, *

the five Platonic solids scaffolding the

universe. All hollow, yes, but hollow

like calyxes for the essential Dream

that seminates eternity, whose faint

bouquet is the "astounding beauty"

Harmonice Mundi raptures over still,

now, in our late December. Over Prague

of the hundred towers, jumbled roofs,

the winter river, the reconciling bridge,

* down our endangered air, forgiving snow *

cajoles the earth

in musical

notes

yet

*

GRAVITY

Mildest of all the powers of earth: no lightnings
For her—maniacal in the clouds. No need for
Signs with their skull and crossbones, chain-link gates:
Danger! Keep Out! High Gravity! she's friendlier.
Won't nurse—unlike the magnetic powers—repugnance;
Would reconcile, draw close: her passion's love.

No terrors lurking in her depths, like those
Bound in that buzzing strongbox of the atom,
Terrors that, loosened, turn the hills vesuvian,
Trace in cremation where the cities were.

No, she's our quiet mother, sensible.
But therefore down-to-earth, not suffering
Fools who play fast and loose among the mountains,
Who fly in her face, or, drunken, clown on cornices.

She taught our ways of walking. Her affection
Adjusted the morning grass, the sands of summer
Until our soles fit snug in each, walk easy.
Holding her hand, we're safe. Should that hand fail,
The atmosphere we breathe would turn hysterical,
Hiss with tornadoes, spinning us from earth
Into the cold unbreathable desolations.

Yet there—in fields of space—is where she shines,
Ring-mistress of the circus of the stars,
Their prancing carousels, their ferris wheels
Lit brilliant in celebration. Thanks to her
All's gala in the galaxy.

                    Down here she
Walks us just right, not like the jokey moon
Burlesquing our human stride to kangaroo hops;
Not like vast planets, whose unbearable mass
Would crush us in a bear hug to their surface

And into the surface, flattened. No: deals fairly.
Makes happy each with each: the willow bend
Just so, the acrobat land true, the keystone
Nestle in place for bridge and for cathedral.
Lets us pick up—or mostly—what we need:
Rake, bucket, stone to build with, logs for warmth,
The fallen fruit, the fallen child . . . ourselves.

Instructs us too in honesty: our jointed
Limbs move awry and crisscross, gawky, thwart;
She's all directness and makes that a grace,
All downright passion for the core of things,
For rectitude, the very ground of being:
Those eyes are leveled where the heart is set.

See, on the tennis court this August day:
How, beyond human error, she's the one
Whose will the bright balls cherish and obey
—As if in love. She's tireless in her courtesies
To even the klutz (knees, elbows all a-tangle),
Allowing his poky serve Euclidean whimsies,
The looniest lob its joy: serene parabolas.

KEEPING CHANGE

Handfuls of change,
Squirreled away, half my life, across
The world, in every strange
City I'd mosey in, a week, a year—
Odd coins I'd pocket, toss
Into a box now flop-eared, straggle here
Strewn on the desk, some crisply cut,
Some thumbed and blunt—flag, owl, ship, dolphin—who knows what?

For years ignored
On their high closet shelf, a stash
Of frizzled racquets, hoard
Of postcards, photos, love notes (old-rose stamp
Her tongue-tip curled to!)—cache
I've spread to reckon with beneath the lamp.
They say "Memento!" and I must,
Leaning to puff away the annuities of dust.

Time's stray parade:
Duce, Reich, junta, *coups de main;*
Legend, adventure, trade;
Copernicus, hula-hooped in star and sun;
At moonstruck keys, Chopin;
The wingèd horse, two breeds: the Italian one
Circus-bred, flighty—off he's flown!
Savvy cayuse the Greek—the hind hooves slash at stone.

Auras of ghost
(Gamy, the old folk's rumor ran,
Like bonfire myrrh, almost)
Rose from dead flesh congealing in its bed:
So, in this graven clan,
What's rotten dies; a fragrance lifts instead:
Mere slugs once for the bought-and-sold,
They're soul's own specie now, her special gloss of gold.

Demonetized
(That's *demon* in a cage, and so
Means evil exorcised?),
Their curse is scoured in time's salt vat, the sea's
—The curse that dogged us, "No
Good thing is ever done for such as these.
Where these insinuate, our face
Changes, and smiles go sly—our mettle too is base."

These innocents
Have quit commodity for good,
Shrugged off the purse-and-pence
To ponder—as lips that pore on lore of lips—
What blessed them while it could,
The fostering palm, disbursing fingertips.
Relics, you conjure far too much:
Ardor our fingers felt, curled palms they burned to touch.

Now Hanukkah
Entwines in fire the Syrian kings;
The romp Veronica
Swirls in a bright bewilderment of bulls.
Hands rummage all such things
For clues: no wonder a djinni in metal pulls
My thought to pole or pole: *when? where?*
We had transaction, once. Our futures, all, cried fair.

The *złoty* here
Means Vistula starlight, bush and bank
In shadow, no one near
But each near, nearer each—that *near*'s a fire
Poor hearts hope nuclear. Thank
This *drachma* then for Delphi: our desire
Raced where the naked runners' sweat
Spattered the sod where once our soft intaglios met.

These *krónur* stand
For thunder in Iceland, what we'd do
In that black-lava land
Volcanoes scrunched. We read volcanoes right.

16

Read them? Well! *were* them too,
Hotel room dancing to our lava light.
That corridor of doors—gone gray?
Pipes from a primal fire heat Reykjavík today,

Won't warm us, though.
Fire's out—that's scarier than *Fire!*
At least the young thought so.
The coins we tossed, fresh-minted, how they spun,
Dates glittering! Dates expire,
And with them all things current in the sun.
Dates love the dust and pile it deep.
Friend, keep your "Keep the change"—change being all we keep.

THE SHAPE OF LEAVES

A premonition in the leaves,
   old words the forest spoke:
For poplar leaf, read *shield of kings*,
   read *testy rogue* for oak.
Catalpa leaf's a perfect heart;
   your linden leaf, baroque.

Here linden and catalpa drape
   arcades where the entwined
Young hopefuls, dazzled with themselves,
   see all through haloes. Blind,
Good souls, they cannot read the leaves
   or puzzle to construe
Why linden leaf's a crooked heart
   and why catalpa's true,
Or why in fall both turn alike
   to show of goldsmith's art,
Compounding treason in the woods
   —the true, the crooked heart—
Then fallen, mould the earth we know,
   root, humus, tufty growth.

Look, lover: on our weathered jeans
   how rich a stain of both.

TRICK OR TREAT

Holy and hokey, Hallowe'en.
That kindergarten of witches in the street,
Skeletons (but with tummies) doorbell high
Piping up, "Trick or treat!"

A hoyden by Goya with her Breughel chum
Scrabbles black-orange jelly beans—then scoots.
—To think I saw *you*, spangled so,
Rouged, in your Puss-in-Boots

Some forty and more years ago!
Memory: the reruns in full color seem
As three-dimensional as *now*.
Could it be *now*'s the dream

We've been bewitched by?—spirited
Into this crinkled skin, this ashy hair,
Starch at the joints—this hand-me-down
Raggedy gear we wear?

We've dealt with clothes before; know well
Just what they hallow, and how they fall away
Strewing the floor in moonlight; yes,
Into and past midday.

Good costumes then. But now let's play
Pretend with those glittering infants at the door,
Now that our autumn's come and soon
The snows arrive—before

We're out of costumes and a place to play,
Of zest for the zany carnival in the street,
Out of breath, out of world and time
Teasing with "Trick or treat!"

FROM THE RAPIDO: LA SPEZIA–GENOVA

Glossies of Eden? The slim beaches curled
Between rocks and the frill of foam—that's when
There's thunder of tunnels and the underworld.

Pitch-black, down Pluto's flue—till out we're hurled
Back to sea-dazzle and tile roofs' cayenne,
To glossies of Eden, to slim beaches curled

Like sinuous Eve, her lassitudes. The muraled
Villas uphill—it's Steinberg heaven!—then
That shudder of tunnels and the underworld.

But swimtogs merry in blue coves! Their swirled
Piquant revealings—glory be! Amen
To glossies of Eden! to slim beaches curled,

Pavilion, pier, a blazon of towels unfurled,
Twined lovers, barmen, kids, a pup—again
A thunder of tunnels and the underworld.

Books talk of Bede's warm hall, how winter whirled
Through wassailing scops—back into night—that wren,
Sparrow, whatever. But these beaches! curled
So close to abutments of the underworld?

IN VENICE, THE LIGHT AIRS

The Apothecaries haue Bookes of Gold, whose leaues being opened are so light as that they are subiect to be shaken with the least breath, yet rightly handled, they serue both for ornament and vse; such are light Ayres.

By gold marquees the iron men tell time
And time tells iron men the way to rust.
Rust?—if the word go rummaging for rhyme
It scuffs what all journeys tumble into: *dust.*
Venice had water once, and has it yet
—Through wrack, and the dusty opulence of gold.
Gold?—loaded word: each resonance a threat
Of winter, age, sad bells. Lives bought and sold.

Airs take you, errant, where you're loath to go
(Every enchantment's coupled with a curse).
Breath moved to *pleasure,* but the lip fussed, *woe;*
Aspired to *better,* but the lip curled, *worse.*
Words stray, like funnel clouds, and trail debris;
Light airs make mockery of the gulled marquee.

WATER MUSIC

'Άριστον μὲν ὕδωρ . . .

"Nothing noble as water, no,
    and there's gold with its glamor . . ."
Pindar on trumpet—First
    feisty Olympian Ode to the horseman,
Daring us, across the years:
Look to excellence only.
Water, you're pure wonder! here's
February, and on the pane your
    frost in grisaille show how you flowered
    all last summer; it
Stencils clover, witchgrass, mullein
    meadow; between boskage gleam
Shores of Lake Michigan, her snow pagoda, junks of ice.
Farther off, spray and breaker, and your clouds
That hush color to a shadow as they pass,
While snowflakes—just a few—go moseying

Around . . . over . . . That cloud-coulisse
    valentine of a window!
Back of its ferny scrim
    scene after scene of a gala performance!
"Water's Metamorphosis,"
That's the show, and in lights too,
Booking all the world for stage.
Now let's make believe there's a magic
    camera, sensitive only to
    water molecules,
Loading film that blueprints hidden
    wetness in things—profile bold
But pearly the pulp of it: highrise, traffic, elm, marquee
Like electronic pointilliste machines;
On sidewalks, prismatic people, prismy dogs;
Ice-palaces for home. They effervesce

22

Of course. Water's alive with light.
  Spawned of the ocean, life's macromolecules
Begot history and time;
  culture their afterthought. Our own
Body: mainly bog. Like
  trees walking? No. Walking waves
Are what *we* are. Flesh briny. Our bone-shack sways
  to, smells of, the sea-wrack.
If we're stormy, halcyon too,
  no surprise, with such
Surf, doldrum, and seiche in us.
  Alcoholic? Some.
Water-freaks? Every last one. (All but death,
Old bonehead who, teetotaling, totals all.)
  Thanks to wet ways, we live here.

You've seen films of the Hindenburg?
  Sky afire and the human
Rain from the clouds? But that's
  hydrogen's way: a psychotic companion
Turning—in a flash—berserk.
As for oxygen: sulphur's
Cousin, arsonist, a false
Friend to metal, apt to explode our
  sleepy haze of sawdust or wheat.
  Sickrooms venture its
Name in whispers. Breathe it straight a
  while, and your throat burns, your head's
Logy, disoriented—you're a weakfish gulping sky.
(Nitrogen-thinned, it's breathable.) We've two
Irate djinns here—and what kabbalahs compel
Their spirits to that peace in H_2O?

Strange, that water's a blend of fire
  when it's flame that she hates and
Hisses, her molecules
  angled like arrowheads tooled for a crossbow,
Blunt, just 104 degrees.
Agincourts in the faucet?

Why not? Hi-tech myths can ape
Many an apeman superstition.
   Yet if not twined lovingly—these
   two explosives—my
Wineglass here could turn *grenade*. As
   water reminds us, the world's
A maelstrom of lava beneath her easy circumstance.
All matter's smouldering at the core. Old-
Time Jehovahs—brimstone and the flood on tap—
Might better have let hydrogen relax

        Its double bond to oxygen—
          which would have shown the folk, given folk to show
        Just who *was* Who, as most
          things evanesced to zero space
       —most, including people.
          Water's out friend. Faucet-flow
        Around finger endears, the way kittens do.
          It blandishes bourbon
        As it mellows (fluid and cube)
          fire to amber, with
        Glass melodies. Diamond, ice
          crystallize alike
        (To the eye); ice though is good-humored, and
        Come spring, will restore playhouse and beach to us,
          melt to mellifluous tilth.

Besides, diamond's a liar—*poof*
   and it's soot when the heat's on.
Calling their glaciers back,
  Ice Ages warmed to us, left the lea greener.
What would Diamond Ages do?
Shrink-wrap countries in rock-glass,
Leave the planet strangled, sky's
Lavaliere, a Tiffany bijou
   glinting frigid fire. And would you,
   Diamond-Age young girls,
Cherish dewdrops, think them jewels to
   pretty your hair with—eyes brave
Through the damp of your lash before the livid avalanche?

Let's be glad—most of us anyway—we're
More dew-sort than diamond-kind. And there's the myth:
What suckled Aphrodite, sea or stone?

Festooned Sicily shore?—where foam,
    all glissando and swell, wreathes
Buoyant the swimmer. Dream:
    eastward in Eden once sparkled a garden
More delicious even than
Sappho's: apples blew perfume
Through liana languors; brooks
Wove their watery spell; mid-grove a
    Presence walked in cool of the day.
    No one dewier
Than that human pair, pellucid
    two, in the sun-flickered shade
By the pools, on a ferny tussock banked like pouffes. No one
Dewier? *You* were! that rickety pier
Once! your shoulders bubbling moonlight as you swam
And then—spirit of water, lithe—gleamed bare

            As moon on the pier, hair swirled back,
                laughing at me, "Last one in . . . !" Prismatic girl
            (Like those glorified trans-
                lunar dancers that Dante saw)
            Sprinkling me with chill lake's
                mischievous fire. Now the tears
            Are like fire to think . . . think . . . what I've thought and thought.
                But safer to think small:
            Summer thunder, hail on the lawn;
                cuddling scotch-and-hail,
            We blessed it as "heaven-sent!"
                Mostly water is.
            Pray that it keep us. Our blue globe in space.
            Our grand loves. Our least ones—like this spindly rose
                rambling on Pindar's lattice.

Alps, island, jet, crest, logo—Barnum's own
Chromos on luggage of the lives we led.
Contessa, in the Mercedes toward Chinchón,
Remember, the day of the bullfight, what you said?—
When, ruffling back your curls' mahogany gloss
(The cub reviewer enthused, "Pompeian torrents!")
You showed me a cheek glass hail had marked, crisscross,
The night your Ferrari was crumpled north of Florence;
And, mocking yourself, emoted, "My 'career'!
My dreams of *Vissi d'arte!* Doomed? In ashes?"
As—I don't think before or since—one tear
Glistened, a moment's diamond, in your lashes,
Gleamed and was gone. Then lightly, "'*Cosa fatta.* . . .'
—Remember Dante? It's true our blossoms blow
Away too early? Except forget-me-not. Ah,
Non ti scordar di me!"
                                    The words we know!
The words we know, to cherish and forgive in,
Console us when their referents go wrong.
Afford, somehow, a sort of world to live in
(So leaden hours are alchemized in song).
Not words to post on luggage. Hardly posh there.
Your palm cajoled my right hand from the wheel,
Lay in it, easy.
                            Later, in the crush there,
We parked, sipped our *anís*—then bugles peal.
Curls—their autumnal luster!—veiled a cheek
Your finger questioned still; eyes twilight-blue
Mused on the crowd, the rough-and-tough, the chic
—Gina was there and, word went, Ava due
Down from Madrid. No bullring, so they made
A planked-in plaza of the village square,
Ramshackle stands that lurched as we ¡*Olé!*'d;
Gazers from rooftop, window, everywhere
And often eyes on you, who'd known that town
From childhood, stranger from your Umbrian hill

26

At first, then friend to many up and down
Those streets, most every fall. And special still.

Nothing went wrong, that day, at the wild rites.
Nothing—that day. We've seen the manshape flung
Dark on the sky for all his suit of lights,
Or from the horn, an endless second, hung.
And we've seen more: death's rubric on the sand
Beneath the sky's wide innocence of blue.
But nothing that day. Still, I kept your hand,
Saw the half sucked-in smile, and knew you knew
Moments of truth too blinding to expect
Unless one wore the initial on her cheek,
His mark, the new possessor, who'd collect
His own in time. His time. We didn't speak
Much in that numbing razzmatazz, that spree of
Dicey heroics. But my sidelong gaze
Felt a remoteness in your soul—as free of
Burdens, concerns bedeviling our days.
Remoteness? Hardly! Not by *sol* or *sombra*.
—Lightness, a buoyancy of hawsers cut
Is what I felt. More aureole than penumbra,
Much as you were, through all the days we—

                                       but
You nudged me, "Nearly over. Let's be going.
Away from crowds." Once through them, with head high,
You led to a *glorieta*—there, boughs blowing,
A flurry of poplar leaves from the loose sky
Hoo'd at us, hustled us, tourbillions pulling
This way and that . . .
                   then, withered,
                             . . . off in wind . . .
Leaves colorful as comics. Luggage peelings
Of island, alp, jet, logo—paper-thin.

THE WINE OF ASTONISHMENT

Thou hast shewed thy people hard things: thou hast
made us to drink the wine of astonishment.

In a cozy booth at noon,
Musky wine our pleasure. Soon,
Touch of finger, touch of knee
Terminals of circuitry
—Long we loll, as in our eyes
Jane and Tarzan socialize.

    One more for the road, and so
    Sleekly overboard we go
    Drifting off amid a kiss
    —Surfers ride a sea like this.

Crowding close (as couplets do
Huddling unheroic too)
Onward we meander, twined.
We're a sight—but never mind.
Look, they circle wide from us,
Homefolk herding for the bus.
Don't they know it's virgin spring?
Know we're put on earth to sing?

    Who says bubbly life goes flat?
    Rites of noon chant, Hell with that!
    Didn't Solomon himself
    Shimmy at the liquor shelf?
    And his tuneful kin take part
    With, "Wine maketh glad the heart?"
    Didn't vivid saints in Spain
    Just to put the matter plain
    Liken love, when most divine,
    To enrapturings of wine?
    (Ours, *de la Grange Abélard*,
    Memories of the mazy Loire.)

Now where are we, you suppose?
Headstones huddle, rows on rows
—It's a marble orchard! Scary?
No, it's grassy, shady, airy.
In their model digs, the dead
Keep their place, with, at their head,
Slabs of data—ups and downs
Mimicking our taller towns.

> Raw geometry, these stones:
> Knob and bobbin, spire and cones
> So unlike what went below—
> Bodies with their to-and-fro
> Sassy amorous ado,
> Curve and curl and—well, like you.

> But these chunky stone-folk? No!
> Never! Not the way to go.

Though no curfew toll the knell,
City sirens do as well.
Trying out a slab for size
Say we sit and elegize.
I'll be tabbed with granite too
When our walkabouts are through?
Well, if weepers come to grieve,
I've some magic up my sleeve:
Underneath this stone doth lie
Nothing that was ever "I"
—Any more than clothes I drop
Off now at some resale shop.

> Odd that, when you think of death,
> You inhale with deeper breath,
> That your sudden heart's a-leap
> With the life it means to keep,

that you're somehow more *alive*.
Odd to think about. Take five.

    And the memories that return!
    Memories that "bless and burn":
    One I kissed by Capri quay,
    One in Yountsville, Tennessee
    —Now, though quay and town decay,
    Nothing shales the kiss away.
    Not that it shot rockets—none.
    More a match-flame in the sun;
    Careful!—not so pale a flare
    That you'd trust a finger there.

Once the tribal tears are shed,
What's death but a change of bed?
Darling, we've changed beds before,
So who minds the darker door?
Didn't lanes of deeper dark
Counsel lovers where to park?

    Tricking out our *death* as *bed*
    Doesn't hold for *dying*. (Dread
    Veils it—chilling and obscene.)
    "Lovely . . . soothing Death" I mean,
    What the good grey poet chants,
    Slop pail in the frowzy plants.

        As for shucking bodies off,
        Dowdiness (ask any prof)
        Comes of wearing entropy .
        —Shake away the stuff! Get free!

Garments flung aside before
Lay at bedtime on the floor,
Lay there as the naked went,
Breathless, to love's stark event.
Things that happened many a night
Led us to the heart of light.
Though I won't say, quite, the Cloud
Of Unknowing. Not aloud.

In your gloriole of curls
Once you woke, the way of girls,
—Breasts, in candor of a yawn,
Like originals of dawn—
Stretching, kicked the sheets away,
Sat up laughing, "Why it's *day!*"

       That's the way it's going to be.
       Proof? I've proof galore in me.

       Further proof before we close?
       Einstein, Planck, de Broglie, those
       Ardent spirits, tuned so fine
       On the headiest of wine,
       Once, in ecstasies of mirth,
       Flicked the seven veils from earth.
       Unappareled, as in dream,
       They saw meadow, grove, and stream,
       Saw our every pleasure spot
       The reverse of what it's not.

       Shucking duds of circumstance,
       Nature did her naked dance.

Einstein, in a fit of glee,
Found a gaudy teaser: *E*
= *mc²*. That *m*
Means our *mass* of flesh and phlegm.
m's why, trying as we might,
We can't touch the speed of light.
m's for *mortal* too—old troll
That's a drag on time and soul.
Flesh succumbing, off it drops
And we're spry as light! Time stops.

       In effulgence of pure *c*,
       There remains—? Elysian *E!*
       Energy at speed of light—
       What a way to spend the Night!

Madcap saint, Teresa, she'd
Tell of *terrifying speed*,
Of *velocidad . . . temor*
In the spirit set to soar;
There's no *bullet from a gun*
Sped like soul at take-off—none.
Bullet? Gun? Castilian truth
Wants *pelota, arcabuz.*
Ávila and Amherst—nuns
Making with the loaded guns?

Speed that's incandescence. There,
All the facts of when and where,
Earth and every common sight
Bonded as coherent light,
Broken symmetries of earth
Tuned in unison. It's worth
Claiming we're forever! So
Blow the moment till it glow.

Even sound and sense concur:
Obit's snug in *obiter.*

Spirits—raki, sake, kvass—
Sing, *In vino veritas.*
Tavern wisdom. Old *da·guerre·o·-
type* of motto. But, *In vero
Est vinositas*—there's truth
With the zingo! zest! of youth.

Our way's rocky. To begin it
Take a truth with relish in it.

Dear? You're miffed? Toe tapping while
Lightnings flicker in your smile?

"You're so funny, love! So phony!
Such an upchuck of baloney.
You a *thinker?* That's your angle?

You—with head all jingle-jangle?
We don't need such hocus-pocus.
Noon put everything in focus.
Muscadet's a lovely laser.
Cat's pajamas. Occam's razor.
In the spring, are lips for talking?
Use them right. Then let's get walking."

   Well . . . *then!* To our cozy booth
   For another round of truth.

CLOSED FOR RESTORATION

Our gaudy years in Italy! In between
Those years and now, some thirty. I'm back today.
Eye, stride (and finger in guidebook) still as keen
—Only, rebuffed by barriers. *Ma perché?*
Brancacci Chapel? The Borromini dream,
Our shiver of pleasure? San Clemente's floor?
The monster's Golden House, weird walls agleam?
All? *Chiuso per restauro* against the door,

Giving us pause. Odds are, I'll never see
That span again. If on Liguria's shore
I lie, *Qui dorme in pace*'s not for me,
Stones with *le ossa* . . . or *tristi spoglie* . . . or
Any such dismal lingo of the lost.
Mine, *Chiuso per restauro*. With fingers crossed.

HOSPITAL BREAKFAST: WITH GRACE AFTER

I

Waking in drifts of whiteness: head to toe
I'm a white sheet, with all but nose below.
Toes ripple, push, make corners; the sheet pulls tight
Until I'm hemmed in a box here, with four right
Angles and four straight edges, as if I lay
Chalky—

    A skirt swirls. And the breakfast tray!

All's orange: dawn at the window, juice I drink.
"Carols of Florida in that golden ink,"
Croons fever, loony. And egg-yolks bobble, most
Like the sun's globe through cirrus. Tussle of toast
That tugs in the teeth. Blonde slinky marmalade—

Lord, what a world the Lord of matter made!

Breakfast—that daily "He is risen!"—swirls
Its color, tang, aroma—cozy as girls
Leaning bare shoulders over, warm hair loose . . .

In breakfast such epiphany? Joy in juice?

II

We, trivial, live by trifles. Froth: our race
Vague as a drift of atoms, in blind space?
Earth offers "neither joy, nor love, nor light,
Nor certitude . . ."

    Was Arnold *real?*

        Not quite.

35

Let's venture—for what's to lose?—a breakfast prayer
To the great Thought that dreamed us—if it's there.
St. Peter once went surfing and he scored
Riding his big feet only—look, no board!
Once, strong souls walked on water; were ultra-tough
Sag-free conniption-proof all-weather stuff.

We're not like those. But, wreathed in gulls and kelp,
Would ruffle the tidal shallows. Peter, help,
Help us to scrabble over wrack and sand
Alongshore toward—

                    some distant lighthouse?—
                                  and

To dangle (though water-walkers all are gone)
Our toes in the froth and glamors of the dawn.

ELEGY

For Marion, for Jane

I

DEATH AND THE MAIDEN

Were you, as old prints have shown,
armor over props of bone,
scythe like scorpion tail a-sway,
here's a word or two I'd say:

When you met that lady now
—her of the amused cool brow—
which of you with more an air
carried off the occurrence there?
Held—the buoyant head so high—
every fascinated eye?
Stole, as half in mischief too,
scenes *you* strutted front to do?

Which at last, when curtains met,
had us leaning forward yet
in the dark?—to breathe and rise,
odd elation in our eyes?

II

"ONE DAY ANYONE DIED I GUESS"

Here she lies, poor dancing head,
in the world we know of, dead.
Every sense avers: The End.
Yet we're hedging (who'd pretend
our five portholes on the night
gauged the seven oceans right?)

hedging: past a world in stream,
past the learned journal's dream
(quark or quasar, beta ray),
what's that glimmer? limbs at play?
Something there? a curtain stirred?
Laughter, far and teasing, heard?

Where such awesome laws are set,
Honey, misbehaving yet?

MÉLISANDE AT THE KALEIDOSCOPE

A versatile fellow fertile in retort—
Though low on sweet talk. Twirl, and you're in Maine
Sea-green with blue of balsam. Twirl, for thunder's
Rolling oath in the lurid gorge of Spain.

Spain's come and gone. Now all's a winter bleakness;
In arctic camps the nervous guy wires whine.
Rose window next. Or cells' embattled sector.
Diamonds bedabbled with dark blood or wine.

Put by that giddy toy. Look to the world now:
Our showboat of roulette wheels, spun in sport
—Glad-handing or cold-shouldering, by turns, till
Who in that swirl knows hurricane from port?

Warmth from such light? that frosted sky, those blinds and
Baffles? that hall of mirrors, heads that talk?
Well, love can blaze *our* way, a fire unknown to
Cellar café and menu scrawled in chalk.

Maybe a clue there, Pelléas? What's light but
Eyeful? Eyes sift—in zigzag bits—each spark,
Sunk in their bony home. A long *Lights out!* then.
Fire, to delight high heaven, needs the dark.

POETRY WORKSHOP (FIRST SEMESTER)

It's time. I find them waiting in the hall.
Sun-burnished Claire, with Jane not plain at all
—She's majoring in glamor. Gloria's here
With Megan, Liz, and Leila. Guenevere,
Already ripe for legend. That's our class.

In skirt or jeans they settle, start to pass
Poems around, assort them. Check their hair.
Then read their verse in turn.

                  It's my despair,
That verse. For some relief, my reason flees
To plan harangues, in fantasy, like these:

"Dear, you start writing, you're an instant hag!
Wizened and blear, spine crooked, feet that drag.
From the crisp lip, what bulbous generality:
You write 'enamored of your personality'
When you mean *love;* for *naked* you write 'clad
In Nature's finery'; call yourself, when *sad,*
'Lost noodle in gloom's soup'; then soar to sing
Paeans to 'stellar orb' or 'vernal spring.'

Must your own words lampoon you—you of all!—
Gawky graffiti on a chapel wall?
Your figure, now, 's in high relief—not flat—
Incised here, and there salient. Learn from that:
Don't write on one dead level: emphasize.
Let your wit sparkle sometimes, like your eyes.
Fine turn of ankle—and why not of phrase?
Lips in live color—and yet talk in greys?

Words should be lithe and lean, compact as muscles
Our marathoners build—not stuffed in bustles.
Thought should be there like bone, that's best unseen;
Emotion run like blood through all. I mean,

Look at yourself: you're classic *Ars Poetica*,
For realms of gold (see Keats) the one right *Baedeker*.
There!—in your looking-glass The Vision's found
(Though here you're fragrant, warm, and in the round).
Study, as Yeats said, what your mirror shows:
Lines elegant with entelechy. Trust in those.
'To thine own self'—see what it means?—'be true.'
Why? To show soul, as all fine bodies do."

But no!—no talking that way. Realler far
Than selves you play-act are the selves you are.
No: you'd be hurt, flick skirts and flounce your hair
—So ponies paw the earth. I see you there:
Head high, you stalk away. Such rhythms flow
As thrill the heart—then break it.

                           So don't go.
Just sit here with me, wordless, and effulge.
I've no more pet opinions to indulge.
Or, talk of what you will. Vacations spent,
Summers to come. Relax and loll, content
To be, if not our laureate, our delight:
The perfect poem none of us can write.

THE CLOSING TOMB

And so it's over. If they meet
   where others peer askance
for clues to the tattled agony
   —just the indifferent glance;
nothing but "darling" tossed aloof,
   the onward cruising eye;
no shadow in the voice to show
   how deep the daggers lie.

Only, as drinks go round and round,
   their eyes across that room
lock in despair: *the orange groves,*
   their candor and perfume!
till blighted by our ancient 𝔓𝔯𝔦𝔡𝔢 . . .
   black letters on the tomb.

PALINODE

So, the well-known gamut run,
  Love, hate, rage, despair,
He awoke one morning, free,
  Breathed a cleaner air.
Bolt upright in bed he laughed:
  Not a phantom there.

Sat and laughed, and whole of heart
  Damned the pale girl then,
She whose beauty broke that heart;
  Damned the careful men.
Hugged his fate that gave a heart
  Time could break again.

Hearts that finish life entire,
  Hearts the rank and sweet
Never cramped in agony,
  Rode roughshod that beat—
What's that thing? A human heart?
  Throw the dogs that meat!

Throw it to the pale girl then,
  Let her pink and blue
Beauty mumble at that rag
  When the dogs are through—

    Cossack, wash that brutal tongue!
      Or go gargle glue!

    Knowing: there were touches once
      —Likely not again—
    Knowing: many a time she left
      All the world of men,
    Curled so close—oh none could tell
      Sobs from kisses then.

What's for comfort? Stout cliché
  That locks lovers tight:
Earth's a whirligig; blue noon
  Riddled with black light;
See the very sun, our saint,
  Waltz with lurid night.

DANTE: AL POCO GIORNO E AL
GRAN CERCHIO D'OMBRA

To waning day, to the wide round of shadow
I've come, alas, and come to whitening hills
Now when all color dwindles from the grasses.
Not so with my desire: no change of green,
So sunk its roots are in the ruthless stone
That listens, talks—you'd think a very woman.

But like the season, this incredible woman
Stands frozen there, a bank of snow in shadow.
The heart within her no more melts, than stone
When softer weather mellows all the hills,
Changing them back from chilly white to green,
The time it nestles them in flowers and grasses.

When round her head's a garland of sweet grasses,
Out of my thought goes every other woman!
So trim they mingle, curly gold and green,
That love comes down to linger in their shadow
—Love that enfolds me in those gentle hills
Tighter by far than mortar holds a stone.

More magic power than any fabulous stone
Her beauty has; its pain no herb, no grasses
Have skill to heal. Across wide plains, through hills
I've fled to escape the glamor of this woman.
In vain: from sun so bright no hope of shadow,
No hill, no wall, no wood's deep leafy green.

There was a day I saw her dressed in green,
And such, she would have driven the very stone
Wild with the love I feel for her least shadow.
How I'd have wished her then, in pleasant grasses,
As deep in love as ever man knew woman
—And wished our field were snug among high hills.

But sooner the low rivers ride high hills
Than this young plant, so succulent and green,
Bursts into flame for me, as lovely woman
So often does for man. I'd couch on stone
My whole life long, feed like a beast on grasses,
Only to see her skirt in swirls of shadow.

Whenever now the hills throw blackest shadow,
With her delicious green the one young woman
Hides all that dark, as summer grass a stone.

NIAGARA

I

Driving westward near Niagara, that transfiguring of the waters,
I was torn—as moon from orbit by a warping of gravitation—
From coercion of the freeway to the cataract's prodigality,
Had to stand there, breathe its rapture, inebriety of the precipice . . .

Fingers clamped to iron railings in a tremor of earth's vibration,
I look upstream: foam and boulders wail with a biblical desolation,
Tree roots, broken oar, a pier end, wrack of the continent dissolving . . .

Braced, like tunnel workers hunching from implosion of locomotives,
I look down: to ancient chaos, scrawl of the fog for commentary,
Misty scripture—Delphic, Jungian—all mythology in gestation,
Mists that chill our face in passing, soar to a mushroom luminescence . . .

In between, where halos dazzle—as, on a high wire, spangled dancers—
On the brink those waters sluice to, in the devil-may-care insouciance
Of their roistering to glory, no forewarning of what impends, till
Solid earth dissolves beneath them; all they had banked on once, vacuity . . .

Kindled in the hollow wind they flare to a greenish incandescence;
Channels they defined so smartly in the gusto of their careering
All behind them now; before them, blinding haze and the noon's diffusion . . .

II

Ten feet over those, our railing perched on a spur where verge and void—there!—
Hiss and arc to touch each other, matter and shadow-matter fuming,
We stare through the flow to bedrock, flashing its Kodachrome geology.
Images swirl by—real, fancied—bits of hallucinated litter:
Gold of oak leaf, taffy wrapper, lavender airmail—assignation?
Yellow Kodak pack, pied comics, tissue a crimson lip had stippled
(Let's imagine). Some shows vivid, fresh-shellacked in the river's sepia,

47

All no sooner seen than vanished—on to the brink, its foaming rotors
Hoarse as all earth's turbines turning in a thunder of synchronicity.
How deep toward the edge? waist? shoulder? as through a woozy lens we scan its
Floor, old temple tesselation—
                              No, terrain of the moon! Medusa's
Ancient face, and we stare frozen: stony glare in its vipers' tangle . . .

Still a thought returns and troubles: "no forewarning of what impends, till—"
Shadow of *impends*—more menace coiled in the word than fact itself has:
Fact erodes in action: Athens, in the arroyos of her theater,
Leaned to watch the self-destructing of her blinded grandiosities,
Willfulness and Will, a crash course; then, too late for it, anagnorisis;
Purged of trivia through immersion in the clotted baths of tragedy,
Then she knew and was transfigured by contrarious exaltations . . .

III

Eyes can't leave the livid seething, its reiterative *Memento!*
Reading, in this bubble chamber, stuff of the world as effervescence,
Reading every life as half-life, reading in foam the one prognosis . . .

Mac the trucker—checkered mackinaw, sort of a baseball cap with earflaps,
Fists to crinkle up his beer cans—here at the falls is philosophical:
"Down the tube. That's life"—he's waggish, nudging his cozy blonde—"You
                                                        know, hon?"
And she knows. We all know: Nature, making a splendor of our banalities,
Lavishes Niagara on us, nudging our knack for the anagogical . . .

Meanwhile, earth itself rolls over, nations caught in its tug of traction,
From the brink of noon to darkness (but the grandeur of the transition!)
Gone, like taffy wrapper, tissue:
                              ferny world of the stegosaurus,
Heraclitus, toe in rivers, Coriolanus in Corioli,
Dancing T'ang girl, belles of Bali, kings of France with the Roman numerals,
Gone, the fripperies and follies glossed in an *Architectural Digest*,
Halls of mortuary marble, dinky glitz of the rare *objet*, the
Aubusson, netsuke, scrimshaw, Tiffany, Tanagra, Bokhara,
All things *au courant*, things current—what a word with the gorge before us!—

All our bookshelves, facts in folio, paleontology, agronomy,
Jewels from that cluttered dump, statistics—
                                        many a scuffed Aladdin's lamp there:
As: one cell's genetic lore'd fill seventy-five Manhattan phone books;
As: for each poor soul among us, many a galaxy out there somewhere,
Each of us more precious—rarer!—than a glittering island universe . . .

We could catalogue forever; there's no end to the world's diversity,
All that affluence from somewhere, more than a continent behind it;
There's no diminution either from the torrential cornucopia
Since that primal burst of fireworks, first explosion from singularity;
All the *things*, their scree, diluvium—go to the malls for confirmation:
Lurid brass shop, teak shop, tech shop, patio 'n' pool shop, campy duds shop . . .

IV

Most we're through with soon enough, but some! how they lacerate the heart—not
Savage indignation's gash—but thrilling, with finer blade, pain's inmost
Nerve: the unsigned card *I love you* kept in a bureau drawer for decades;
Sweater she wore once, that autumn, rich with the campfire musk; then letters,
Lavish *o*, impulsive flourish, "When you're away, in other cities,
It's their weather reports I look for, first thing in the morning papers . . ."
So once the Provençal poet, in his rapture about *freid' aura:*
"Winter winds that blow from your land
                                    feel like heaven upon my cheek here . . ."

They've gone too, Provence and poet, off in the jumble-carts of history,
Who was *she?* that rueful beauty, jewel of the court and joy of kings, who
Dying murmured, "Je me regrette!"—wistful dear, with her curls disheveled
On that last of all her pillows, feeling the dark impend—"I'll miss me!"
Images swirl by: châteaux that dance in the pool's hallucination,
Fêtes and follies effervescing—champagne, glass, and the hand that held them—
Last, herself, the self where soul is, world of her lavalieres and lovers.
Did she dream, through mists arising, how on the high wire, floodlit dancer,
She had lived her brilliant moment? Hear, as the blood ran hushed, sonorous
Thunders of the living river, more than a continent its source? And
Not divine—so near the brink where verve like hers and the void meet, seething—
Wreathed in opulence of sunset, some transfiguring of the waters?

Notes

THE SIX-CORNERED SNOWFLAKE

In 1610 Johannes Kepler was living not far from Týn Church in Prague's Old Town (Staré Město), the section to the west of the Vltava River. One day, crossing the famous Charles Bridge—begun in 1352 and, with its great bridge-towers at either end, still a tourist attraction—he noticed the snowflakes on his sleeve and again wondered, as men had for centuries, why they were always hexagonal. In views of Prague at the time we can trace the rest of his walk: passing through the Little Quarter (Malá Strana) at the far end of the bridge, he began his climb up to the heights of Hradčany (*hród-chany*) and the palace of the Emperor Rudolf II, the reclusive and eccentric collector of great art and of curiosities of every sort—among them his master of ceremonies, the painter Arcimboldo, who did the emperor's portrait as an assemblage of fruits, grains, and vegetables. Kepler had come to Prague some years before at the urging of the astronomer Tycho Brahe, who, having lost his nose in a duel, had replaced it with the gold and silver one which it is said he kept dabbing with an ointment he carried.

Kepler's wonderment about the snowflakes led to his writing a charming little book in Latin, *De Nive Sexangula*, as a *Strena* or New Year's gift for a patron. In it the author, who knew the classics well enough to write poetry in Latin, does quote Euripides. Elsewhere, on more than one occasion, he quotes Persius, one of his favorite poets. Kepler of course had no way of knowing what we know now about snowflakes: the single flakes are hexagonal because of the molecular behavior of freezing water. But he has some witty and original observations about their form and about form in general. The poet who "lyricked" the lines quoted in stanza 11 is Francis Thompson, in "To a Snowflake."

Stanzas whose shape imitates that of the object they describe go back at least to the ancient Greeks, who called the practice *technopaignia*. Often they are little more than what that name means: "technique-play." But sometimes, as in George Herbert's "Easter-Wings," in which the lines expand and contract with the thought, the shape itself can dramatize what is being said. Thoughts about snowflakes and their shape seemed to offer the once-in-a-lifetime chance to make use of what is graphic in typography. Technical specifications: in the hexagonal stanzas, the three equal axes between opposite points intersect in 60-degree angles at their center.

WATER MUSIC

Somewhere in the course of my thinking about doing a water poem, what is probably Pindar's most famous line came into my head. I looked up the rhythm of the ode in which it occurs, wondering if his complicated Greek meters could be transposed into our accentual system. English writers (like Goethe and Hölderlin on the continent) had adapted the more familiar Greek meters, but I could not think of anyone who had taken the prosodic pattern of a Pindaric ode as the metrical substructure of a poem in English. It was a challenge: interest in form is more adventurous if one tries to do new things with it. As Pound knew, one way to "make it new" is to resuscitate something so old that everyone has forgotten it.

The "Pindar's lattice" on which this poem is grown is the quantitative-syllabic grid of his "First Olympian Ode," with the long and short Greek syllables transposed to our accented and unaccented ones. Key rhythmical elements are the *glyconic* (x x — ∪∪ — ∪ —) as in line 1, and the *pherecratic*, a catalectic form of the *glyconic* (x x — ∪∪ — —), as in line 6. (The *x*'s mark syllables that are "common," either long or short.) Other rhythmical elements are related to these. All are forms of *logaœdic* or "speech-song," combinations of dactyls and trochees felt to be somewhere between prose and verse. The meters of individual lines vary within what we might call the stanzas; corresponding lines in the 16-line strophe and antistrophe have the same meter. The 15-line epode (every third "stanza," indented) has its own pattern. Some sequences that work out in Greek cannot very well be carried over into English: line 13 of strophe and antistrophe, for example, begins with seven short syllables in a row. In English seven unaccented syllables together are unlikely, or probably even impossible, except in some such jokey line as "'B-b-b-b-b-b-b-but . . .' he stammered."

One advantage of using such an accentual-syllabic grid is that it offers the writer the best of two worlds: to a listener (or reader) his poem may sound as free as prose, but to the writer comes the satisfaction of knowing that he is following, syllable by syllable, accent by accent, a form as rigorous as the chemical affinities of nature are.

NIAGARA

The rhythm of this poem was suggested by the galliambic meter of Catullus 63 (a translation of which, in galliambics, may be found in the third edition of my *Sappho to Valéry: Poems in Translation*, University of Arkansas Press, 1990). The Latin poem, though its content has nothing to do with "Niagara," is worth recalling here for its own sake. In it, Catullus gives us his version of the story of Attis, the Phrygian fertility figure that corresponds to the Syrian Adonis. Attis, in a fit of religious mania, castrates himself for the goddess Cybele—and lives to regret it. As

Frazer writes in *The Golden Bough*, "When the tumult of emotion had subsided, and the man had come to himself again, the irrevocable sacrifice must often have been followed by passionate sorrow and lifelong regret. This revulsion of natural human feeling after the frenzies of a fanatical religion is powerfully depicted by Catullus in a celebrated poem."

One thing that caught my interest in the poem was its curious rhythm. Gilbert Highet, in *Poets in a Landscape*, says the meter is "fantastically difficult . . . the rhythm of the eunuch's savage dance, on which he plays many subtle variations. . . ." L. P. Wilkinson, in *Golden Latin Artistry*, says, "The Galliambic meter was invented to express . . . the orgiastic dance to Cybele—the essentials beneath the variations are the anapaestic tread of the wild dance and the short rattling syllables of the tambourine or castanets at the end." The meter is, basically:

$$\cup\cup - \cup \mid - \cup - - \mid \cup\cup - \cup\cup \mid \cup\cup \stackrel{\cup}{-}$$

Catullus takes the usual metrical liberties: two shorts for a long; a long for two shorts, reversed syllables, etc.

For years, probably for two or three decades, I had been teased and haunted by this rhythm, wondering if, with its quantitative basis changed to our qualitative one, it could be made to serve any purpose in English. The only poem I knew that did try it in our language was Tennyson's "Boädicea," which the poet said was a "far-off echo" of the galliambics of Catullus. Because of the meter, he published it among "Experiments." With lines that speed up at the end, it does have the feeling of the galliambic movement, but Tennyson does not try consistently to follow its pattern.

I am not sure how "Niagara" first fell into this rhythm. I may have been attracted by the sweep and amplitude of the long line. At some point I came to think the meter appropriate for my subject, since in a way the poem is concerned with, among other things, solidity and dissolution. After the solid first half of the line, the second half seems to rush away in a flurry of quick syllables. These had forced Catullus into using or even making up words not found elsewhere in Latin: *hederigerae, properipedem, sonipedibus, nemoriuagus*. They invited too the polysyllabic words toward the end of many of my lines, which differ metrically from his in that I have added an unaccented syllable at the end of the line to lighten the second half still further.

Afterword: Some Notes on Form and Formalism

Oh! quel farouche bruit font dans le crépuscule
Les chênes qu'on abat pour le bûcher d'Hercule!

The preceding notes describe how one can make use of a relationship, real or fancied, between the subject of a poem and the form it takes. Besides the poems I have mentioned, a glance at "From the Rapido: La Spezia-Genova" will show how the form (villanelle) was suggested by recurrences in the journey itself: brilliant scenes of ocean, cove, and villa alternating with the abrupt blackness of the many tunnels along the Riviera. As for "Tide Turning" (in an earlier book), there was perhaps something crotchety in my thinking that the six hours of the changing tide warranted the sextuple structuring of the sestina, a form I had not previously had recourse to. In "Water Music" the connection between form and content was more tenuous: a mere phrase of Pindar.

This relationship, like any other, can be abused. Only the good sense of the writer will tell him that "Ode on a Grecian Urn" need not be written in urn-shaped stanzas or "Ode to a Nightingale" in some kind of wingèd ones. Solidity and dissolution are physical qualities or processes and as such may have an affinity with the physical dynamics of verse. Just *may* have. But this is by no means true of other subjects. The theme of recurrence happens to fit the recurrence-template of the villanelle. But since there are far more themes and shades of feeling than there are literary forms, such pairings are rare indeed.

Of course it is desirable to have the expression of a poem in sympathy with its subject; that way form corroborates content. But meter and stanza are almost never mimetic and are seldom adapted exclusively to what they say. Shakespeare and others have used the single form of the sonnet for themes as different as youth's eternal summer and lust that is perjured, murderous, and bloody. Emily Dickinson, through all the range of her emotions, was generally satisfied with the commonest of quatrains. The same form can serve numerous purposes. Perhaps all we mean when we say that form should be appropriate is that it should not call attention to itself as inappropriate, as dissonant from what it is saying, unless dissonance is its message.

Recently there has been a resurgence of talk about form and formalism. There is much to be said for the first of these terms, somewhat less to be said for the second. Poets should probably be wary of enlisting under any *-ism;* they should be doubly wary of anything that, like a General Motors product, has to proclaim itself as "new."

The word *form* has a variety of meanings, some of them antipodal. For the philosophers *forma* can mean *soul,* the in*form*ing principle that animates whatever is alive and organizes whatever is not. But for most writers *form* is more likely to mean *body* than *soul,* the body of words informed by the poet's thought and feeling: the texture of imagery, metaphor, symbol, color and sound of words, their connotations and ironies, their rhythm, the spatial and auditory features of their presentation, and all of the devices that rhetoricians have cataloged over the centuries.

This is form in its fullest and richest sense. But generally when we speak of form and formalism we limit our understanding to its most obvious elements; to meter and the patterning of line and stanza. This limitation is useful for discussion, but, if it becomes too grim a fixation, it can be ruinous to the spirit of poetry. That is no doubt why the word *form* has been in disgrace with many writers over the last couple of decades. Some seem to think that the function of form is like that of a cookie-cutter. And indeed it is in some of the duller formalists; reading them one is inclined to nod in agreement with what Roy Campbell had to say "On Some South African Novelists":*

> You praise the firm restraint with which they write—
> I'm with you there, of course:
> They use the snaffle and the curb all right,
> But where's the bloody horse?

No one has paid more honor to the supremacy of form than Paul Valéry. In his remarks on Victor Hugo he quotes the "excellent formula" of Mistral, "the great poet of Provence": "Form alone exists. Only form preserves the works of the mind." Valéry expands the formula: "Form alone can indefinitely guard a work against fluctuations in taste and culture, against the novelty and charm of works produced after it. . . . A writer may, in his day, enjoy the greatest favor, excite the liveliest interest, and exert immense influence: his final destiny is not in the least sealed by this happy success. It always happens that this fame, even if justified, loses all those reasons for existing which depend only on the *spirit* of an age. The *new* becomes the *old; strangeness* is imitated and surpassed; *passion* changes its expression; *ideas* become widespread; *manners* worsen. The work that was only *new, passionate, significant of the ideas* of a period

* *Collected Poems,* vol. I, The Bodley Head, London, 1949.

54

can and must perish. But, on the contrary, if its author has been able to give it an effective form, he will have built upon the constant nature of man, on the structure and function of the human organism, on life itself."*

Strong medicine for all but the most stalwart! What lesser aspirants would not sell their soul to "enjoy the greatest favor, excite the liveliest interest, and exert immense influence . . ."?

Valéry has much to say, here and elsewhere, about the versification and music of poetry, about its need to "sing" rather than just move its lips. He tells how, in his own experience, form would sometimes precede its subject: how his mind would be possessed by the music of a certain rhyme scheme, line length, stanza form *before* he knew what the poem was to be about. From such an apparently perverse process would result some of the greatest poems of the century. This may remind us that in Shelley's manuscripts some stanzas were left unfinished except for the rhyming words, words that would provide the structure of a stanza not yet clear in his mind.

In my own case, form was not something I was converted to or seduced by. I did not, at some time in my life, become a card-carrying formalist; form, for good or ill, was something I was born to. In caring for it I was faithful not to a literary movement of the '40s or later, but to the sources of poetry as I felt them in those primal intuitions which are, many poets have felt, "the fountain-light of all our day."

A few years ago, in a note "On Growth and Form"—the title from D'Arcy Thompson's classic of science—I explained it in this way: "From the time I was five or six, I thought poems were a part of the natural world, as real certainly as the rabbits and collies we kept. All the poems I had known throbbed with a physical rhythm, had what is called *form*. Form is what I thought poems came into the world with, as plants and animals do. Poets, I might have said if given to such talk, have to be careful about how many feet they put into their lines, just as nature has to be careful about how many feet she puts on her own creatures: six for insects, four for animals, two for the likes of us. I probably would have thought 'tetrameter' quite as natural an organism as 'quadruped.' Nature, producing all of her works in this shape or in that one, perpetually delights in the forms she proliferates. With every new discovery, science seems to confirm her preference. It was Murray Gell-Mann, Nobel laureate in physics, who observed that 'if we compare the creation of ideas here [in nuclear physics] to the writing of poetry, then we have to write sonnets, and not free verse.' It was a professor of theoretical physics, Paul Davies, who in 1980 marveled at 'one of the great mysteries of

* *The Art of Poetry*, translated by D. Folliot, Princeton University Press, 1958, p. 254.

cosmology': the fact that the universe is highly symmetrical and its expansion isotropic. 'Out of all the . . . chaotic motions with which the universe could have emerged from the big bang, why has it chosen such a disciplined and specialized pattern of expansion?'"* I took comfort in such remarks as those of Gell-Mann and Davies. Surely one's aesthetic preferences cannot be all bad if they are in sympathy with the universe?

Even as I am writing this, in the first January of the last decade of the century, I see a headline about the new spacecraft COBE (Cosmic Background Explorer):

EXPLORER SEES UNIVERSE THAT IS NEARLY FLAWLESS

The article explains that "evidence so far shows an expanding universe much smoother and more uniform than most scientists had expected"—a universe, that is, even more like "formal poetry" than had been thought.

A universe symmetrical, disciplined, even flawless? Perhaps the early universe was, but we know only too well what turbulence has come into it, most of it of our own devising. Can form cope with the disorder of existence? We know that it can: in Aeschylus, Dante, Racine, Shakespeare, there is no horror their formal prosodies cannot deal with. Though the primal meter is flawlessly regular, turbulence comes in with the passionate human rhythm that breaks and rides it. In any classic trimeter, hendecasyllable, alexandrine, or pentameter, there is room for the turbulence of the universe.

> Cover her face. Mine eyes dazzle: she died young.

Webster's eleven syllables have a prosodic turbulence close to the kind of chaos that interests physicists today—though the listener whose ear is attuned to (or untuned by) nothing but amorphous verse may be quite insensitive to such violent subversions of prosody.

Talking about such elements of form as meter and stanza can be hazardous; it may give the impression that their importance is of a different kind than it really is. The virtue of a poem does not consist in its exemplifying this or that meter, stanza form, or typography. These matters are ancillary; what is paramount is the communication of deeply felt human experience. Unless that is communicated, meter and the rest are frivolous; a costive devotion to them is a kind of pedantry.

And yet we might feel that "ancillary" is too modest a word for these formal elements. I remember Robert Fitzgerald once saying that rhythm is the *soul* of poetry. If we don't wish to spiritualize it, we might at least say that rhythm is its breath of life.

*"On Growth and Form," in *Selected Poems*, University of Chicago Press, 1982.

For it is through these elements that poetry comes into being; they are its *sine qua non* if not its *ne plus ultra*. One might say they are like the scaffolding at a construction site, meant to be thrown away and not regarded once the building is completed. In part that image of scaffolding is an appropriate one. Formal concerns do help in the construction of a poem: a writer with a form in mind knows in what direction he is going and at what pace; he knows too that he is working toward a finish line and cannot maunder on forever, but, like a wise marathon runner, must measure out what breath he has.

But since the prosody remains embedded in the finished work as scaffolding does not, a better image is that of the armature in a statue: an essential part of the finished structure. We do not judge a statue by its armature, any more than we judge a beauty contest by the X-rays of the competitors. But what the X-rays show is essential to beauty; without the armature of the skeleton Miss America or Mr. Universe would collapse to a heap of flab—as much of the spineless magazine-verse of our day has done. But there is an opposite extreme too: some verse of other eras, and even of our own, has been known to present us with the fleshless bones of formalism.

Probably one reason that some writers today prefer the amorphous to the shapely (except in games they play and creatures that they love) is that form smacks of the elegance they have been taught to disdain—elegance was outlawed in the intolerant '60s, together with many other excellences. Yet that same elegance is what our physicists prize as a mark of truth in their theories and equations. The Chinese-American Nobel laureate Chen Ning Yang refers to "the intrinsic elegance and beautiful perfection of the mathematical reasoning involved" in the laws of symmetry. We can think of more than one recent poet who, if told he should work for "intrinsic elegance and beautiful perfection," would have booted his well-meaning advisor out of the room with a burst of profanity, of which he had a better command than of metrics. I am not talking, of course, about the languourous elegance of the haut monde, but about the sinewy elegance a mathematician sees in an equation, or that we see in such poets as Sappho, Catullus, Villon, Donne, Landor, Yeats, Marianne Moore, and many another. Indifference to it is what has given us the typical magazine-verse of our day, which aims at being reader-friendly, common as Kleenex and as disposable. How few of these poems remain comfortably at home in our memory, as once poems vitalized by a rhythm did—by any rhythm, Pope's rhythm, Whitman's rhythm, Pound's rhythm! Such poems seemed to memorize themselves, with no effort on our part, so akin is rhythm to the workings of the brain.

But there are hopeful signs that the ineptness of what I have called the typical magazine-verse of our day is increasingly coming under attack from "the new generation of American poets," as represented, for example, in the recent anthology *Under 35* (edited by Nicholas Christopher, Anchor Books, 1989). Amid the surviving free verse, we find many poems that show more concern for form than would have been fashionable ten or twenty years ago. The once despised pentameter, often with rhyme, is recovering its resonance. Such fixed forms as the sonnet, the sestina, the villanelle, the pantoum are again coming into their own; in poem after poem one sees an inclination toward stanzaic symmetry on the page. In *Ecstatic Occasions, Expedient Forms* (edited by David Lehman, Macmillan, 1987) a number of "leading contemporary poets select and comment on their work," with more attention to such matters as the function of prosodic technique than we would have found in the anything-goes decades we have suffered through. More than one poet is moved, as Mona Van Duyn is, "to say something on behalf of the for-so-long-beleaguered formal poem," though not all are as outspoken as she: "I can freely leave an unfinished free-verse poem to prepare a meal, sleep, have a drink with friends, but a formal poem follows me everywhere, makes me hard to live with, and gives me pleasure approaching the ecstatic."

We can be happy then that all is not lost, not even in a world in which everywhere the eloquence of speech is belittled by the electronic raree-shows that more and more ensorcell us with phantoms.